ALSO BY DAVID MILLER:

Tesserae, Stride Publications, Exeter, Devon, 1993
True Points, Spectacular Diseases, Peterborough, Cambs.,
    1992
Pictures of Mercy: Selected Poems, Stride Publications, 1991
W. H. Hudson and the Elusive Paradise, Macmillan, London
    & St. Martin's Press, New York, 1990
Darkness Enfolding, Stride Publications, 1989

STROMATA

David Miller

STROMATA

Burning Deck
Providence

These texts have appeared, in part or in their entirety, in the following journals: Eonta, The Poet's Voice, Room, screens and tasted parallels, Shearsman, Sow's Ear, *and* tel-let.
"Messages" was originally published as a pamphlet by Torque Press, in 1989.

The cover reproduces two monoprints by Andrew Bick.

This project is in part supported by grants from the National Endowment for the Arts in Washington, D.C., a federal agency, and the Fund for Poetry.
Burning Deck is the Literature Program of Anyart: Contemporary Arts Center, a non-profit corporation.

Library of Congress Cataloguing-in-Publication Data
Miller, David, 1950
    Stromata / David Miller.
       p. cm.
    Contents: Stromata — In the field — Moments — Fire water — Messages.
      ISBN 0-930901-96-7 (pbk. : $8.00)
      ISBN 0-930901-97-5 (pbk. signed : $15.00)
      I. Title.
PR9619.3.M47S77 1995   94-38655
821--dc20   CIP

To the memory of Edouard Roditi

CONTENTS

STROMATA

BOOK ONE

Sitting on a coil of rope, he watched the man fall asleep on a map large as a blanket. The map tore with the man's turnings; pieces were blown into the dark waters.

■

—There was a painter who lived in an island hut, painting at night by a dimly-lit kerosene lamp.

—Almost in darkness...

—He didn't look at the paintings in the daytime. And when he saw them exhibited in galleries...

—Under artificial lights...

—...he'd often denounce them as forgeries.

■

Standing at the sea's edge, waiting for the rain to break, I think of that day we walked together along the mudflats by the river.

She sang the melody without any embellishment; her voice "true," drawing the lines of song through the air.

There was a plant fragment (polypody) caught in her hair. —Don't move, I said; just for a moment.

■

—Figures of infinite regress bore me but *not* him.

I caught the sentence and missed its meaning, my attention more on other things: the fire that had been built from planks and branches; the wine being passed around in paper cups; the two little girls wrapped in their blue sleeping-bags, both girls white-faced after a dip in the cold night sea.

■

A man tells his companion of rituals involving fire and binding (knots, webs). The girl is small and thin; in her middle teens. The man's older. They walk over a bridge, down a narrow walkway, then another walkway; it's dark and there's a strong wind, and this entire riverside area appears empty of other people. She says to him, laughing, Is this where you turn into a monster, now? He walks away from her. She shouts, Bastard, fuck you!, but the man, already at some distance, in the gloom beyond the street-lamps' reach, doesn't answer. She shouts again, her voice tearing: Is it over then?

■

Not even the reed-mats' lines, white powder of decayed material; nor the smashed adornments of "the small princess" — fragments of gold decorations belonging to one so young that her death left her unaccompanied, entailing none of the sacrificial killings familiar to the excavators.

A perfected abandonment.

— The eye sees stone, and sees nothing. The wall is quite literally a wall, to which the young woman presses her face, her body shaking as she weeps.

■

During a holiday abroad, my friend sent me a postcard about seeing a film at an open air cinema, "to the accompaniment of jets landing at the nearby airport, and with the underwater photography mostly washed out by poor projection and too much extraneous light."

He returned; and one evening we stood together and talked, in the small garden at the back of his house, while the darkness settled. He spoke of the long illness and death of a mutual friend of ours: before these events, he said, it had seemed that similarity, even uniformity, had been most important to him — in persons as much as in nature.

■

Dear —,

It was too quick for a dream, nor was I asleep as I stood there, having closed the door behind me, and about to switch on the lights. For an instant, a girl was crouched in a corner, sobbing.... And when the lights were on, and I saw that the room was empty, a voice, only just audible, kept calling my name. It was as if the pain you'd related of your adolescence, twenty years in the past, suddenly woke in me. Coulisses? Nothing in the room took on such an aspect; there was nothing there by which I could save myself.

■

A man sits in the dark; listening, nostalgically, to a recording of nature sounds. I don't; I think of a friend, a much-admired older poet. I think of when we sat talking in a café near his hotel; and of how later that day I wandered alone through a park, trees uprooted from the storm of two nights before, each thought of his voice breathing calm upon the air around me. The very sound in memory was my refuge.

BOOK TWO

Sitting beneath the almond tree in blossom, I watched a little girl, the delight in her face simple and frank, skipping the rope held by another girl and an old man.

The dark came, and with it the lighting-up of the streetlamps bordering the park.

(Later:) I listen to Chet Baker singing *Imagination* and *My Foolish Heart*; the voice tender in its candour. "Colour so fragile"... it seems "as if it could be blown away."

■

—....and did you know that your painter crossed
the Timor Sea on a raft, starved and hallucinating at
the end of the voyage, his obituary already printed?

But those and other details about him had been
with me for many years; and I'd once written:

> A lone man on a raft
> crosses a Sea. Imaged face
> becomes almost the shape
> of a paper lotus-petal —
>
> we remember the dead with prayer
> and dream, equally those we love
> who will die. Paper lotus-petal:
> flickering lines across its surface.

■

She stretched over the couch where I was sitting,
to pick up the glass of wine on the floor. The arch of
her back, the small nakedness between blouse and
skirt. In the vertigo born of an upsurge of longing,
sight momentarily emptied itself out. — Between her
writing desk, and mine: so many ways of saying.
(Sitting together at a table in the flat that belonged
to her absent friend, she'd read her poems to me
from the characters that appeared on the small dark
blue screen. Her voice composed the details of a
mimesis "derived," as Gadamer says, "from the
star-dance of the heavens.") — And if I look up to
see threads of snow falling in my room, like the sea
that Su Tung-p'o woke to, where his floor had
been...?

■

I was working for a time in a late night bookshop, located — curiously — in a seedy garment district. I was there once during a storm, reading and listening to the rain and the long rolls of thunder, when an acquaintance came through the doorway, dripping water onto the floor.

—Beware young women who believe they're in contact with statues, he said. —A gift for delusions, he continued; sitting in that museum day after day, communing with the damn things.

Looking out the window, I remembered:

> ...blood soaks into the carpet
> under bare feet.

— but not thinking of him. — There was a window in the poem, with two people standing at it.

> ...What sea
> have we come to, it strikes
> the smallest thing: *the radiant heart.*

■

You leaf through the book, looking at the way the colours of the letters are displaced, black by red, for pages.... Misery's singular, however many the lives it possesses; and though assigned to marginalia, its images impoverished, powerless — it claims me in you, claims succour; and I am claimed utterly; so that I take place through this dispossession.

■

—I dreamt I took my children's bones from their graves, washed them, fondled and kissed them... and I awoke raving, with the sun.

—But you don't have any children, I said.

—Yet there was something..., he said; something that held me.

(He'd seen my friend waiting at the bus-shelter, in a memory borrowed from a single photograph; whereas I, long familiar, was rendered invisible.

(Sitting in the disused bear-pit, my two companions and I drank to the spirits — we said — of the dead bears. Later, we saw the remains of the old rheumatology clinic, now mere rubble. And following a path isolated in light, came to a mausoleum covered with scratched inscriptions, the angels' faces mutilated.)

■

A friend writes: I'm sitting here, out of the heat, thinking about what you've written regarding the human image. How could one *ever* be able to paint another person, I've asked myself....

Another friend: We lift the group of bones, with the earth in which they're found, as one mass — which is then encased in a layer of plaster of Paris.

— *Dream folding into waking life and back into dream, and within those folds, the strands of yourself tearing apart.*

■

Dear —,

If I think of what is most terrible in a life, the life of someone I love, it is almost entirely unsayable. Unless it is a matter of testimony, how can you say it? Let alone write about it: for personal histories are not "usable"; even though they may be drawn upon, if respect and reticence are the keys to a distinction.

My sister wrote to me, "Do you still paint? I hope you do, because you were too good to stop. The picture of a girl with red hair you did in pastel is lovely." — Not only had I stopped — I couldn't remember any such picture; nor even working in pastels. But whatever the medium of portrayal, I can only approach the idea of imaging another human being with something akin to fear....

Yet in what's said and written and shown, there is always this possibility: time itself called to judgment.

■

He pulled the large drawings out from beneath his bed to show me. Colour, as well as imagery, had been displaced. But I thought of Izutsu: "Black here is not sheer black. For in its negation of all colours, all colours are positively affirmed."

This man, the artist, works in daylight; I write in the evenings. I like to think of Rilke, when he was Rodin's secretary, writing at night, the lamp in his window signifying work done in the night; and the young Cocteau seeing that light, but not knowing for many years that it was Rilke who'd occupied the room.

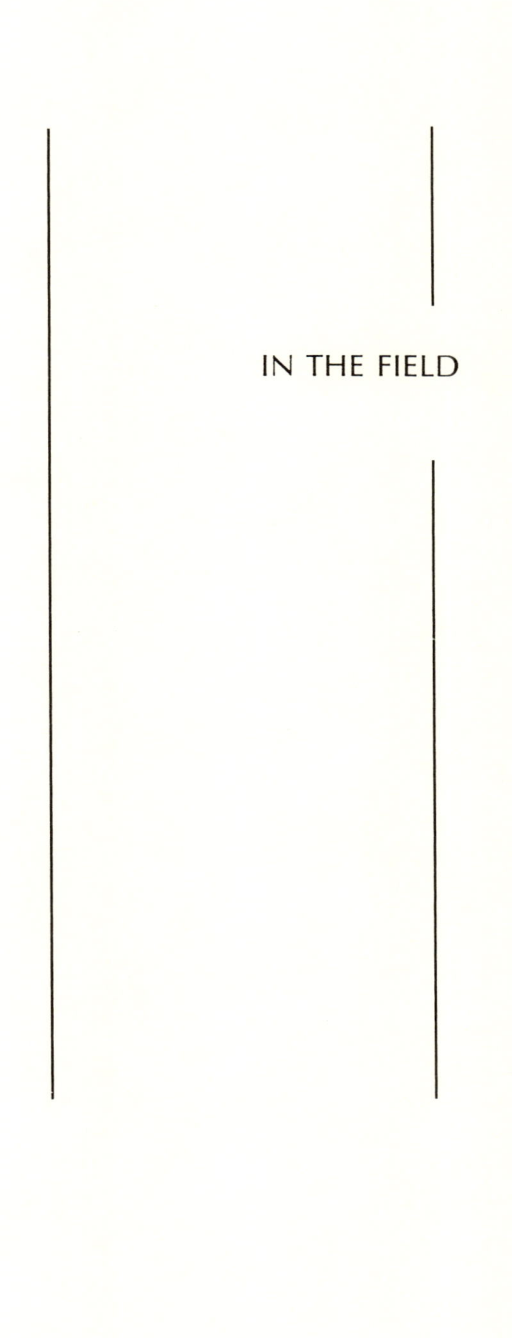

IN THE FIELD

1.

'don't turn away where are you gazing
and whatever are you gazing at?'
'there was a huge golden man'
the girl said 'lying down on a couch
and the couch was in a field'

2.

details reproduced through layers levels
the dream coming home in day's hours

3.

a line in vermilion
brushed onto paper
gold body-colour
anticipations of black
on white revealing birds
and immortal beings

4.

'throughout that field there were outbursts
of crying' but the children take on the aspect
of celestial nymphs and a love
from before birth's remembered
unearthly life stirring in faces

5.

and the tribute which he offered
was a picture of the Lord of Heaven
and of the Mother of the Lord
altogether improper things he brought bones
of supernatural beings they are superfluous things
which ought not to enter the palace

6.

disseisin *where were we now*
where else could we be
than in that same field

MOMENTS

Graph of durations: grid on which we move. Cut each line on the grid down, down to where thought stops. *When a line is cut into many parts, no matter how many the parts, something will be left. One can never cut into the last unit.*

■

'The hare will never conclude the race which is his love — each moment is divided, cut down further, closer to impossibility. He runs and is still.' Ah yes; my hand reaches toward you, reaches and will not reach. Yet even in the photograph, how evident that water has already bathed the wound.

■

Perhaps it's that very moment when the child raises her head, with its shock of auburn hair, to look up at the sky; a look that's immediately cancelled by the sun's too-intense brightness.

Or perhaps it's another selection of time, not an afternoon's blue, but a dawn completely red, orange. Cry out in the midst of it.

FIRE WATER

(For Gerhard Richter)

1.

shapes of dream moving beneath

what tone what
tones black white grey

2.

windows smashed
row of windows
rows of windows
odd-shaped holes to look out of
faces appear in corners

hacked, smashed, blown
out of air
the mixture of
elements

she dyed her hair and
cut it, rearranged it
there are photographs to show this
"change of appearance"

one of the men had eleven
disguises
they are documented in
eleven photographs

the woman, Gudrun, was
arrested·in a boutique
after a shop assistant
spotted her gun

cool air of the morning

all those dreams
apocrypha
the night just as it was, but
out of that

bullet in the arse

Shining back, flowing back
meditative face, the
high cheek-bones, long face
roundness of the cheek-bones
tight but lovely line of the lips
toughness
lines of the neck

she was found dead in her cell

another was shot in the eye
by police

"A time (he said) is quickly approaching

the eye the eye

"when the privilege of immunity for the
"crimes of the ruling class

lines of the neck

"and their henchmen...
"will disappear..."

"News is sold as a commodity, information
"as a consumer product

the target in the wind, the lines
of force

"— what's not consumable must make them
"vomit"

3.

each night
wet with thin rain

for those who pass in
and out of the rooms
one room the tree
in near-dark

How the ethical gazes out
irrevocable, from iris and pupil

MESSAGES

The corona in this dark is your being's (mouth pressed tenderly upon mouth). Sending a kiss, I duplicate the sign of unlettered identity.

■

The shapes of interpretation rise up at the borderline between stasis and flux. I trace the oppositions and equations, negations and similitudes; my hand does not cease in the labour.

∎

In the stops and breaks of her story, the evening concentrates her glances; her young voice edging towards maturation, tells me in clear tones, "I disappeared from all their lives then," *tabula rasa* which the circulating lines of desire trace, and trace over, and over.

∎

Daylight hours were spent asphalting the roads
and streets. Black ink ideograms filled the rest of the
time: reversed to white in the heart's dictation.

■

What is it which we, looking at each other, can
only translate, imperfectly, into longing — into
words expressive of longing? — Unity, which is not
"beyond good and evil," but rather the "beyond" of
good and evil — the transcendence implicit, posi-
tively, in good — as its fulfilment; and in evil — as
its negation.

■

As in a dream: knowledge bleeds into fore-
knowledge of fresh atrocities the dead walk back into
corrupt skins, telephone their orders of butchery
again.

■

—If you've gathered the flames about you and
locked the doors, to die with your signs; how bitter
the ecstasies then.
—Melodrama isn't extinguished in café small-talk
— in its so-ordinary semi-darkness; but in the vic-
tims' insistent claim to be heard.
So he seemed to say; and so I thought; and we
talked around these things, sitting in a café, looking
out at the columns of piled stones in the street.

■

Looking out or looking in: the portico and the door
and window are flames. Hands gesture in talk, the
fingers spread; the voice catches; and the face, given
into my life, endures.

STROMATA by David Miller
Errata:

P. 26: for "group" read "groups"
P. 54: insert semi-colon after "atrocities"

This book was designed by Rosmarie Waldrop in 10 pt. Century Schoolbook, with Optima titles. The cover reproduces two monoprints by Andrew Bick. The book was printed on 55 lb. Glatfelter (an acid-free paper) and smyth-sewn into paper covers by McNaughton & Gunn in Saline, Michigan. There are 1000 copies, of which 50 are numbered and signed by the author.

BURNING

For more information contact:
Rosmarie Waldrop (401) 351-0015

DAVID MILLER
Stromata
Poems, 64 pages, offset, smyth-sewn
ISBN 0-930901-96-7, original paperback, $8
ISBN 0-930901-97-5, pbk., signed, $15
Publication date: September 1, 1995

Miller is a phenomenologist. He sifts and resifts the lessons of perception, of "raw" experience, in order to open them into more complex compounds of vision, emotion and thought. He probes the human story, the sensuous world, and a range of philosophical discriminations with the aim of defining just what it means to be alive and think.

David Miller was born in Melbourne, Australia in 1950 and has lived in London since 1972. His recent books include <u>Darkness Enfolding</u> (Stride, 1989), <u>Pictures of Mercy</u> (Stride, 1991), <u>True Points</u> (Spectacular Diseases, 1992), <u>Tesserae</u> (Stride, 1993), and a critical book, <u>W. H. Hudson and the Elusive Paradise</u> (Macmillan & St.Martin's Press, 1990). A book of interviews and articles on his work, <u>At the Heart of Things</u>, has been published by Stride in 1994.

"David Miller's odd and fierce visions dreamed, imagined, composed, are hard as reality to accept except for the completely credible tenor of the poems that shore up, reflect, connect and attract an encouraging spiritual fact..."--Guy Birchard
"Miller is a scholar-poet, a reader of both Book and World, a seeker of truth whatever the enormous semantic and philosophical problems associated with such an enterprise..."--Kris Hemensley
"David Miller searches for the ineffable, for indices of being (not W.C.Williams' "ideas") among things. He is phenomenologist rather than semiotician. The codes are to be broken (apart) rather than decoded, since we cannot know what it was that was encoded in the first place."--Robert Sheppard

Distributors:
Small Press Distribution, 1814 San Pablo Ave., Berkeley, CA 94702
Spectacular Diseases, 83b London Rd., Peterborough, Cambs.PE2 9BS
Collected Works, 238 Flinders Ln., Melbourne 3000, Australia